Germany

A Guide to the Must-See Cities in Germany!

By Sam Spector

Table of Contents

Introduction

Hi, my name is Sam and I first of all want to thank and congratulate you for purchasing my book, 'Germany: A Guide to the Must-See Cities in Germany!'

Germany is an amazing country filled with fascinating historical locations and a deep, vibrant culture. Each of the cities in Germany offers something different to its visitors: from the exciting, colorful beer halls of Munich to the fascinating culture of Berlin. All are unique in their own way, and have different sights and attractions to explore and enjoy.

The German people are often reserved but extremely kind. As you visit each new city you will find that the locals take to you with a warm smile and an open heart, and will often be eager to help you when you look lost.

What I hope to achieve in this book is to provide you with a reliable guide on exactly what to see in each of Germany's major cities, and how to navigate your way around the country to see as much as humanly possible.

I will give you the top ten of my personal favorite things to see and do in each of the top ten cities in Germany, as well as a description of exactly why you simply can't miss them. I will provide insights that I've gained from my own extensive travel throughout

Germany, and some tips for making the most out of your own German trip.

I wish you the best of luck with your future travels and want to thank you again for purchasing my book. Never stop traveling and always seek to discover the unknown.

Chapter 1: Frankfurt

Frankfurt, most likely, will be your first stop on your German adventure. Why? For one thing, because of its central location, it is the perfect starting point for a round trip of Germany (and Europe in general)! As a result of its centrality, overseas flights are cheaper into this metropolis than any other city in the whole of Germany! So, if flying into this booming, boisterous city anyway, why not take a quick look around before you set off on your whirlwind tour of the rest of the country?

Being one of the largest business districts in Germany, Frankfurt has a lot on offer as it has become a center for European finance, where people can go to start a business or conquer their respective professions. You'll witness skyscrapers towering above you as men and women in business attire bristle past you, hurrying back from their lunch break. You won't get the feeling that this is just another metropolis, though, with people here seeming genuinely excited to be going to work every day: they'll pass you by with a brisk stride, a broad smile upon their face and even a friendly greeting of 'guten Tag' (good day) extended your way.

If you're beginning to draw conclusions that this city means nothing but business, think again. Frankfurt also boasts a title of one of the world's most livable cities, with an astounding variety of museums, beautiful parks, a bolstering student scene, exquisite public transport, fine dining experiences and a roaring night life.

The Top Ten

To begin your sightseeing in Frankfurt, the first stop you should make is to the Main Tower. Although this is one of the main towers in Frankfurt, marked as the fourth tallest, it gets its name instead from the Main River! Despite not being the tallest tower in all of Frankfurt, it makes up for it with its unobstructed views and its stellar positioning, making it the best spot to gaze out over the city. From this position you should be able to get a good bearing of where you are and plan out the rest of your adventuring through Frankfurt.

Being the financial capital of Germany, you can't come to the city without at stopping by the Frankfurt Stock Exchange. Deutsche Börse AG's Visitor Center allows you the opportunity of visiting the trading floor in action. It's a far cry from the hysterical shouting, hand waving and emotional outbursts you've probably seen in movies, but it's a great experience nonetheless. Another famous attraction presents itself out the front of the Stock Exchange in the form of two large, formidable, bronze statues: the Bulle und Bär (Bull and Bear). The two statues represent the ups and downs that the Stock Exchange experiences on a daily basis.

Römerberg is an area you won't soon forget, being the historical heart of Frankfurt and center of the Altstadt (Old City). The central square paints a beautiful portrait of olden day Frankfurt, with the oldest section of the Town Hall, the Römer, completing the image. In the very middle of the square sits the goddess Justitia, atop the

Fountain of Justice, facing directly toward the Römer, allowing none to escape her gaze.

For lovers of the performing arts, the Alte Oper is a venue not to be missed. A former opera house and current concert hall, it was destroyed by bombs in 1944, but came back with a vengeance upon its reopening in 1981. Although not the prestigious home of opera it once was, today it has a lively, enthralling program home to all kinds of entertainment.

Poetry buffs will deeply regret not seeing the next attraction, the Goethe House. This establishment was the family home of Johann Wolfgang von Goethe, arguably one of Germany's greatest ever poets and lyricists. Even if you aren't into poetry at all, touring the Goethe House represents a great opportunity to step back into 18th century German living.

The Palmengarten, located in the Western District, holds the title of the largest botanical gardens in Germany. It boasts a magnificent array of plants and flowers, and spanning over 22 hectares, there's plenty to explore - just be sure not to get lost! On a sunny day it's the perfect place to go for a wander around, have a picnic or admire its beautiful gardens.

There exists a special treat that Frankfurters like to claim as their signature drink, namely 'Apfelwein', or as they prefer to call it, 'Ebbelwoi'. This delectable drink is a light alcoholic apple cider which comes from the regions surrounding Frankfurt. The best place to find this specialty is in the district of Sachsenhausen, which possesses some of the best and oldest cider taverns in Frankfurt.

Das Museumsufer is an embankment to the south of the Main River which presents itself as a central hub for all museum lovers. Go for a stroll around this area and spend your day popping in and out of museums. Two of which I strongly recommend visiting are the Museum für Moderne Kunst (Museum of Modern Art) and the Städel Art Gallery.

One thing I love to do if I get the chance in a new city is to visit one of their university campuses. The reason being a lot of campuses own some of the most amazing architecture and beautiful ground in their respective cities. The Johann Wolfgang Goethe-Universität Frankfurt am Main represents one of such campuses for Frankfurt, with its impressive buildings and wide, open grounds being well worth a look around.

Lastly, there exists a nearby town which has maintained its medieval style buildings for centuries and which draws a myriad of tourists from around the world. A day trip to Rothenburg ob der Tauber will feel like a trip back in time as you wander down its delicately preserved streets and marvel at its quaint, olden buildings. Be careful if you decide to visit here, because you might not want to leave the fairytale you've entered!

Chapter 2: Heidelberg

Going by geographical location, Heidelberg should be the next stop for your German wander lusting fulfillment. Located just south of Frankfurt, many travelers I know of chose to bypass this smaller city on their trips, which I believe is a gross mistake on their behalf.

Heidelberg represents what can either be a romantic, picturesque setting, or an awe-inspiring city which will fill you with a yearning to travel back in time! Its Baroque style Old Town is definitely one of the highlights, but for such a small city this place is packed full of plenty of adventures just waiting to be had.

The Top Ten

One of the most notably jaw-dropping structures in this majestic city is the Kaiserdom Zu Speyer (The Speyer Cathedral). This building is of Romanesque architecture, and stands out if nothing else for its sheer size amongst its surroundings.

The Alte Brücke (Old Bridge) is without a doubt a standalone attraction. Spanning all the way across the River Necker, it provides a remarkable viewing point out over the water, across to the city and most spectacularly up to the Heidelberg Schloss.

The River Necker which passes beneath the bridge is an attraction in itself. If the weather allows it you can head down to the riverside park on the North side of the river for a picnic! You'll often find many locals hanging around here if the sun decides to poke its head out from the clouds for the day.

The Schloss (castle) itself is simply remarkable. Perched atop the mountainside, gazing up at it from afar is rewarding enough. When you travel up there and walk its grounds by foot, this is when it becomes a truly amazing experience.

Nearby to the Schloss sits the church of the Holy Ghost, another massive structure of nearly equal magnificence. It's positioned directly in the middle of the market place in the center of the old town, which allows its towering steeple to dominate the skyline of the town.

A few minutes out of Heidelberg, and well worth the trip, is Neuberg Abbey. This Benedictine Monastery is today still home to many monks and is an amazing area to visit, even disregarding the actual building confines.

Heiligenberg represents another chance to witness the remains of some ancient monasteries. Situated to the East of Heidelberg, it contains ruins dating back to around 1000AD among other structures, and also presents another great view over the area.

Heidelberg is another city which has an impressive university campus. The Ruprecht-Karls-Universität, although not the largest campus, is in fact the oldest university in Germany, and as a result has some of the most glorious buildings in the country.

Although within the confines of the campus, I count the Botanischer Garten of the Universität Heidelberg as its own attraction with a jungle of orchids, ferns and all other variety of plants to view.

If this doesn't satisfy your appetite, the nearby city of Mannheim has a campus which is equally as impressive, and presents the perfect reason for a day trip from Heidelberg.

Chapter 3: Stuttgart

This power city is well established as the motoring capital of Germany, and to many others as the car capital of the world! With a long history of car manufacturing and production, and being the home the first ever petrol engine, its important role in the motoring industry cannot be questioned.

Because of this remarkable history, and its contribution to the economy of Germany as a whole, this alone is enough reason to visit the city. With its motoring magnificence aside however, Stuttgart also is a great place to visit with a friendly atmosphere to the whole city. It has one of the lowest crime rates in all of Germany, as well as the lowest unemployment rates.

The Top Ten

There are two obvious attractions that simply can't be missed if visiting Stuttgart. The first is the Porsche Museum, a true experience of motoring excellence which no car enthusiast should miss out on. You can witness Porsche models right from the beginning of their production until the present day.

The second which is just as obvious and just as enjoyable an experience, is the Mercedes-Benz Museum. Though the building's design looks like a spaceship from the future, the experience itself will take you all the way back in time to the invention of the first petrol engine and its production, as you'll be enthralled in the history of this car producing powerhouse. You'll also be lucky enough to witness some vintage cars that predate your grandparents.

From cars to trains, get yourself to the Hauptbahnhof's Aussichtsplatform (viewing platform) right at the top of the huge building! From up here you'll get views reaching out all over Stuttgart, including a different view of the prominent, pointy Fernsehturm (TV tower).

For another astounding view from a different perspective, traverse to the top of Birkenkopf (Rubble Hill). Surrounded by beautiful forest and trails for both walking and biking enthusiasts, it has historical significance as well. While it looks like a simple, grassy knoll, beneath the surface are the remnants of thousands of buildings destroyed in the war, acting as both a memorial and warning for future generations.

More beautiful, fresh, green surroundings can be found within the Wilhelma Zoologisch-Botanischer Garten - an interesting hybrid of zoo and botanical gardens. The gardens have it all from animals and a petting zoo to vibrant flowers and large tree ferns.

A few minutes outside of the main city can be found the peaceful Max-Eyth-See. This lake is a popular destination for Stuttgarters on pleasant days, as although the water isn't ideal for swimming, there's plenty of opportunity to either paddle atop the lake or bike around it.

Heading back into the heart of Stuttgart and into the main plaza, Schlossplatz, you'll find a gaggle of people at any time of the day. With several fountains, a tall statue of the winged Concordia and the regal Neues Schloss (New Castle) all within view; you'll have plenty to look at.

Just around the corner you'll find the captivating Staatsgalerie: one of the most visited museums in Germany. The museum hosts a wide array of 14th to 21st century European art, but one of the most impressive features is the building itself. It's a colorful, playful, piece of architecture that you should not miss!

As if it's landed from the same extraterrestrial planet as the museum, the UFO-shaped Mercedes-Benz Arena is another highlight you should not miss. If you get the chance definitely head here to watch the local team, VfB Stuttgart, play in front of a roaring home crowd.

Finally, if you can escape the city for a day (or even two) then travel South-West to allow yourself to be immersed within the murky depths of the Black Forest. A fifteen minute walk from any major campsite will leave you surrounded by lush, dark evergreens. You'll encounter hills, rivers, vast expanses of dense forest, and if you're unlucky you might stumble upon the Wicked

Witch! Just be sure to leave jelly beans behind you so you can find your way back.

Chapter 4: Munich

Immerse yourself in rich, Bavarian culture as you stay in the city famous for all the right things: beer, sausages and lederhosen. This is one city where I'd recommend trying to aim for the right time of year, that time being around the start of October.

If you can time it right you'll get the chance to experience one of the most exciting and jolly (or gemütlich as the Germans love to call it) parties in the entire world: Oktoberfest. This three week period from September into October is when the city truly comes into its own, with men and women lining the streets and beer halls in their respective dirndl and lederhosen.

Understandably not everyone can make it at this time of merriment, nor may they even want to for fear of it being too crowded, but fear not because this highly traditional city has exciting attractions and activities for anytime of the year.

The Top Ten

When in München, do as the Münchners do! If you really want to get the traditional Bavarian experience, I recommend buying yourself some traditional Bavarian clothing. A dirndl or lederhosen will make you look and feel like a real Münchner as you drink many Maß (liters) of beer. As they are quite expensive, I definitely recommend simply renting one out for a night, that ought to give you a good enough experience without coughing up the $200 to own one!

Continuing with the tradition, book a table at the world famous Hofbräuhaus. This renowned German beer hall is "das Original und das Beste" when it comes to both beer and food! Treat yourself to a few Maß of beer, alongside some Weißwurst (white sausage) and Brezen (pretzels).

Königlicher Hirschgarten is another world renowned beer and food venue, as it holds the title of the largest beer garden in the world! With over 8,000 seats to choose from, you'll have plenty of people to be jolly with, as you heartily drink and sing into the night.

Your time here can't all be eating and drinking (unfortunately), but luckily there are some other great things to see. The Deutsches Museum is one of them, being the largest museum of science and technology in the world. This place is definitely a geek's heaven, and always has cool exhibits to view.

From a geek's dream to a motor head's dream, BMW Welt will make any car enthusiast drool. Step in and get up close to the newest BMW models - you can even get behind the wheel if you like! Try not to get too disheartened when you have to step back out though.

For a little taste of history and some exquisite Baroque architecture, check out the Nymphenburg Palace. The building itself is massive, and the Palace grounds are equally as impressive.

Football fans be sure to get to the Allianz arena, either for a game or a stadium tour. Nicknamed the Life Belt and Rubber Boat, the stadium has walls made from inflatable cushions to can change color to match the team playing. With FC Bayern constantly at the top of the national league, take any chance you can to get tickets to a game.

To get some fresh air and stretch the legs, don't look past the sprawling Englischer Garten. This expansive park is bigger than both London's Hyde Park and New York's Central Park, so has plenty to see and do! One of the most unique things about this park is its artificial river surfing! Go to watch locals jump onto and artificial wave, surfing for as long as they can get away with before another surfer slaps their board in annoyance. If you're brave enough hire a board and test it out yourself!

A little bit further out from Munich exist a lot of great places you can make a day trip. One of which is to the enchanted Neuschwanstein Castle. As the inspiration for the Disney movie Beauty and the Beast, it's even more magical than you can imagine!

For a more educational and stirring experience, a day trip to the Dachau Concentration Camp is certainly worth it. The 'Academy of Terror' was the original training ground for the brutality that spread across Europe during WWII, and a tour of the camp will certainly put things into perspective.

Chapter 5: Dresden

The devastating effects of WWII were felt all over Germany, but there are certain places which experienced more devastation than others. This desolation has been reconstructed and most cities have now fully recovered from the losses they established during the time. There are still some places, however, where you can witness firsthand the destruction and consequences the war had.

Dresden is one of these places. The clear geographical split between the New City and Old City allows you to contrast the differences between the two, as well as fully observe some of the remnants of the bombing of Dresden. Blackened buildings are littered throughout the Old City, and as you stare up at the charred stone you can almost imagine the terror that the flames which once engulfed this city must have wrought. This city is a truly amazing historical location, one in which you'll have the best chance of comprehending the effects of the war.

The Top Ten

The first thing you should do upon your arrival, before you visit anywhere in particular, is to wander around the Old City. Wandering aimlessly through the streets and cobble stone roads will allow you to appreciate the blackened, burned buildings more than if you're in transit to a particular location.

On your way around the Old City, if you feel that you've wandered enough and haven't stumbled upon it already, try to locate the Fürstenzug, or Procession of Princes. Lining the entire wall of an alleyway, it represents the world's largest porcelain mural, depicting the many rulers of Saxony.

If you make it to the outskirts of the Old City, along the river banks, you'll likely have discovered Brühl's Terrace, fondly known as 'The Balcony of Europe'. This architectural ensemble provides both a picturesque view across and along the banks of the river, and a chance to walk along the length of the walls of the former city, where guards would have been posted to protect it from enemies.

A mere few steps down from Brühl's Terrace is the Frauenkirche, one of Dresden's most revered symbols. The original church was destroyed in the war, but the current one is in the exact image of the first. The altar itself is truly remarkable, being reassembled from the nearly 2000 pieces it was obliterated into from the bombing.

Around this beautiful landmark are a series of al fresco dining areas for you to satiate your hungry belly, after all the walking you've been doing. Most leave you with great views to admire as you eat.

Another Baroque style gem which can be found within the confines of the Old City is Zwinger Palace. Built early in the 18th century, this sandstone palace is beautiful from each side and from every angle.

One of Germany's most famous opera houses, Semperoper, is another marvelous structure with centuries of history behind it. This neo-Renaissance prized building had a brilliant life until WWII, before it was shut down. It wasn't until 1985 that music once again filled its grand hall.

Before you crossover from the Old City to the New City, take a little stroll along the banks of the Elbe River. Walking down the length of it and across a few of the many bridges that join both sides will allow you to get a few more viewing points of the many spires, towers and domes of Dresden, as well as helping to contrast the two sides of the city.

Now you can allow yourself to enter into the New City, and into a different world of Indie bars, pubs and stores. The best time to explore this area is at night, as you can hop your way through bars and beer gardens. I recommend limiting yourself to one drink at each, as there are a few to get through!

Out of everything you will have seen so far in Dresden, this final attraction will certainly be the most whacky! The Kunsthofpassage is a cute and artsy passage in the New Town that has some interesting cafes and handmade shops for you to peruse through. It may take a while for you to find, but this hidden gem is worth it!

Chapter 6: Leipzig

A quaint city, with a little over 500,000 inhabitants, Leipzig's contribution to many fields of the arts, particularly to music, have earned it greater recognition than many other cities of larger size. With several famous artists including Goethe and Bach once calling Leipzig home, it represents one of the more significant cultural centers of Germany.

The city is also famous for being the starting point of peaceful demonstrations against the communist regime, which ultimately led to German Reunification and the dissolving of the USSR. The dissolution of communism hit the city hard, but it has managed to recover its economy well over the last few decades.

The Top Ten

The main contributor to the movement which led to the downfall of the East German government was the Church of Saint Nicholas. The peaceful prayers, which are still held today, empowered local citizens to confront the injustices that were rife in their country. Here you can witness the peaceful processions that ultimately saved a nation from such injustices.

The Gewandhaus concert hall is the home of the Leipzig Orchestra, the oldest symphony orchestra in the world, and a building with astounding acoustics. It is now the third Gewandhaus constructed since the original, and is a fantastic option for a night of entertainment.

One of the newest and most special attractions Leipzig has to offer is the fully engaging Asisi 360 Panometer. This 360 degree panoramic wonder is an initiative of the visual artist Asisi, who utilizes a former gasometer to create a giant reconstruction and portrayal of the world. Past exhibits have included a bird's eye look from Mount Everest, a look into Ancient Rome, the depths of the Amazon Jungle and the aftermath of the Battle of the Nations (in which Leipzig itself played a central role).

A sight which pays even greater homage to this last event, and one that rightly draws a huge tourist crowd, is the Monument to the Battle of the Nations. Standing at an impressive 300 feet tall, it is a massively impressive structure, from the top of which you can get a breath-taking view out at some of Leipzig's countryside. The monument was paid for mostly by donations and the city of Leipzig, and commemorates the defeat of Napoleon's conquest for all of Europe.

A little further south of Leipzig sits the Cospudener See. Like so many of the lakes in the region, it sits in the position of a former open cast mine, not that you could tell from looking at it. The lake possesses long stretches of sand to relax on and a wide expanse of deep, blue water.

There's even a sauna available for use directly at the lake!

The Botanical Garden of Leipzig is another natural wonder, dating all the way back to the 16th century. It is the oldest Botanical Garden in Germany, and one of the oldest even in the world. With over 7000 different species of plants and free admission, this attraction is one not to be missed without good reason.

For music lovers, the Bach museum will surely be a highlight of your trip to Leipzig. You could spend all day here, as you listen to compositions of his music at different stations throughout the museum, follow the guided audio tour and view some of the instruments that were used in Bach's time.

Moritzbastei is the only remaining part of the ancient city fortifications. It's not a tourist attraction as such, however, but an entertainment venue! You can get great food throughout the many underground rooms here, and the many little bars represent a meeting point for a lot of the young crowd in Leipzig.

Entertainment of a different variety can be found at the Leipzig Red Bulls stadium. The reasonably new home team, RB Leipzig, have shot upward through the various divisions and seemed to improve each year, now representing a formidable force in the world of German football. They've attracted a fervent fan following as well, but matches are vary family friendly with a lot of them being alcohol-free events, with Red Bull being substituted to rev up the crowds.

The last attraction is a small distance out of the city of Leipzig, but presents a worthwhile day trip. The city of Weimar is significant for its cultural heritage and importance in German History. It played a key role in the German enlightenment and was home to many of the writers who shaped the literary genre. The city also had a leading role for Nazi Germany, as it was the foundation place of the Weimar Republic, and many of the first concentration camps were first established around this area.

Chapter 7: Berlin

This fabulous city is a contradiction to itself in many ways, being the center of both high life glamor and gritty, underground scenes. As the largest and most famous city in Germany, it possesses a truly vibrant culture, wild partying scenes, delicious multicultural foods, astounding architecture and one of the richest histories of any city in the world.

You'll be mesmerized as you walk the streets of Berlin, explore its many dive bars, explore its iconic sights, meet its diverse range of inhabitants and allow it to continue to surprise you with its unpredictability! The whole city is like the canvas of its people, with creativity oozing from every crevice. The abundance of space, cheap rent and exciting lifestyle encourages youth from all over the world to make Berlin their home, as they experiment with their ideas and taste the fruit of personal freedom.

This is not a place you'll be criticized or critiqued for wearing a particular outfit, saying something out of context or suggesting an outrageous notion: this is a place you can truly be your own self as you discover, explore and thrive!

The Top Ten

To truly understand Berlin first you simply have to explore. You'll discover that the city possesses a very diverse range of areas, as you travel between run down, impoverished suburbs to more recently gentrified neighborhoods, within the space of a few steps. Some of these areas have become hipster havens, with many hip cafes and bars to stop in at as you wander the streets. Forget the maps - go explore.

If you happen to get hungry, you won't stay this way for long. This multicultural metropolis is home to numerous cuisines from every corner of the world, the most prominent of which hailing from Turkey. These immigrants brought with them the famous Döner kebab, which has become more synonymous with Berlin living than it is with its Turkish heritage. For a mere few dollars you can get one of these tasty, meat filled rolls which will fill you up enough to carry on for the remainder of the day - if you can still walk after eating it.

As you walk into the heart of the city of Berlin you'll start to recognize some of the icons that Berlin is most famous for. Museum Island is the best place to begin your touristic sightseeing, as you join to the hub of visitors meandering from one sight to the next. You can visit one or all of the five internationally recognized museums sitting atop this island, before setting out to view the other iconic structures.

One of the most impressive of which is the Berliner Dom. This cathedral has been through the wars, literally, and you can see this firsthand from its blazoned spires and walls. The view from the top provides an extraordinary view towards some of Berlin's other notable sights, but even peering up at the Dom from the grass covered square below provides an amazing sight to behold as it stands out from its blue sky backdrop.

The Holocaust Memorial illustrates both Berlin's creativity and somber past, as it pays respects to the many Jewish lives lost throughout WWII. The memorial is made from stone columns which are raised up to different heights, between which you can walk. It feels like a bit of an optical illusion when you're in there, as even the ground you walk on isn't level.

Two of the most recognized and highly visited tourist hot spots have not yet been covered on our tour of Berlin. The first is the beginning location for most of the free walking tours that are taken through the city, and a focal point of the city itself. The Brandenburg Gate, built on the site of a former city gate, is a representation of the solidarity of the German people's resolve, and of European unity. It has also hosted many famous speeches and is now a must-see for any traveler stopping in Berlin.

The second absolute necessity to any German city tour is the Berlin Wall. To Berliners the remaining pieces of the wall represent the conquering of freedom over oppression, and leave a reminder to all others of the extreme travesties that befell East Germany before the falling of the Berlin Wall. It is marked with colorful, artistic graffiti from one end to the other, and even disregarding its powerful historical significance, presents a great attraction to visit. It's so moving that I guarantee you'll feel the urge to visit it more than once during your stay in Berlin.

If you're after some fun things to explore that are a little more off the beaten tourist track, look no further than Abandoned Berlin. With a website dedicated to the many derelict, graffiti-covered, vacant buildings left to rot around the outskirts of Berlin, you should have no trouble finding a few to explore. Some personal favorites include the abandoned ballroom, pool house and of course the abandoned theme park! Just be careful with this last one, as security guards are known to roam the grounds!

Forget about New York - Berlin is truly the city that never sleeps. With what is arguably the best clubbing scene in the entire world, you'll be hard pressed to find a reason to go to bed any night of the week. The clubbing scene is a vital part of the city's cultural blood flow, and even if this isn't really your scene, I recommend checking out some of the warehouse sized parties on offer. Berghain is the most prestigious of the bunch, and probably the most eclectic, but this doesn't mean it's easy to get into. The bouncers seem to have no prejudices except for their spur of the moment decision whether you'll be allowed in - after your hour or so waiting in line.

Lastly, if you can't bring yourself to do one more night of hardcore clubbing, or your body just needs a simple reprieve, there's a perfect venue to mellow out and feel some artsy Berlin vibes. Das Edelweiss's Tuesday night jazz jam sessions provides the perfect atmosphere for such an occasion as the house musicians rock out together for the first hour, before it's a free for all thereafter. Get there at 9:30pm for good seats and before the bar gets too crowded!

Chapter 8: Hamburg

From the largest to the second largest city in Germany, this Nautical haven presents a piece of maritime history simply teeming with charm. 'The Gateway to the World' as it has been boldly nicknamed, Hamburg has enjoyed a rich history of trade with the rest of the world, which has seen it rise to be one of the most affluent cities in the world, and one of the most livable.

With one of the biggest harbors in all of Europe, and more canals and waterways than you can imagine, this 'Venice of the North' is a sea shepherd's dream. It's hard to escape the call of the ocean, as the city's maritime culture is infused within everything you'll see; the food, architecture, music and even the people.

The Top Ten

With more bridges than Amsterdam and Venice combined, allow yourself to cross the many canals weaving through the city as you make your way to the esteemed Hamburg Harbour. Soak in the maritime charm of this great port with the salty smell of the water, mesmerizing image of the gleaming, blue water and the titillation of your imagination by the movements of the many marine creatures that call this place home.

To fully experience the sheer size and importance of this great expanse of water, take one of the many port cruises that are popular for tourists of all backgrounds. You'll get to circle around and see up close a few of the 13,000 ships per year which call into Europe's second largest port. You'll learn of the economic importance of the port to Germany as well as the cultural significance and its shaping of the city to what it looks like today.

Once your cruise of the harbor is at an end, get yourself over to the Hamburg Fish Market! Here you can have a tasty seafood lunch, peruse the fresh fish on offer, or even to put a bid in for any one of the range of knickknacks and assortments being traded at the century old Auction House. In summer many go here for a source of entertainment, with some people beginning their drinking festivities as early as 8 in the morning!

If you can't find what you want at the market, perhaps you'll be able to find a bargain down the Mönckebergstraße. This is the main shopping strip in Hamburg with all of the big names and stores, including both Europe's largest electronics market and Europe's largest sports store! The strip, commonly referred to simply as 'the Mö', also contains some of the city's most interesting buildings, so is well worth a look-in.

To learn more about Hamburg's love of the ocean, you simply must visit their number one museum. With a whopping ten exhibition floors, the Hamburg International Maritime Museum emphasizes Hamburg's powerful connection to the sea and provides an informative look into Maritime history, even if you're not a Maritime enthusiast!

An attraction which is popular amongst all children and grown-ups alike is the Miniatur Wunderland. This amazingly realistic model railway, one of the largest of its kind in the world, will have you jumping up and down and giggling like a little kid as it whirls past.

For something targeted more towards the adult crowd, make your way toward the infamous Reeperbahn, Hamburg's very own seedy red light district. Being more of a tourist attraction than other cities' red light districts, no street girls are allowed on the Reeperbahn itself, although you'll find prostitutes beckoning to you from behind their windows at every hour of the day.

Following a stroll down the Reeperbahn, you can treat yourself to a taste of Hamburg's revolutionary music and clubbing scene. The underground feel of most of the larger clubs, such as Tunnel, are famous for their influence upon and recreation of the house, techno and trance music genres. You can feel that you're part of the next frontier into musical experimentation all while your boogieing your way into the last minutes of the night.

If you prefer the sunshine to lasers and strobe lights, then the Alster Lakes will be the perfect spot for you to visit. Located directly in the heart of the city, the Alster provides the perfect spot to throw a Frisbee, go for a jog or simply kick back on a deckchair. Just don't try to dive in, as it's a mere 2.5 meters deep! During some colder winters you might even be able to walk all the way from one side to the other without getting your feet wet!

The second beautiful, outdoor wonder which is lovely to visit at any time of year is the Planten un Blomen. This park is alive with flowers, ponds and plants, and even has a spirited fountain which lights up in every color of the rainbow as it dances to the music that accompanies it.

Chapter 9: Düsseldorf

Fashion, architecture, the high arts and a zinging night life are all a part of everyday life in this affluent city. As a financial powerhouse, the everyday citizens of this wealthy city may seem at first to be a bit snobbish, but as you stroll up the River Rhine or barhop your way through the 'the longest bar in the world' within the Altstadt, you'll quickly realize that they love to let their hair down once the working day is done.

Some of the older areas in the city have recently been transformed into intrepid and eclectic neighborhoods for the more nonconformist type crowd. Individuals of more refined taste, on the other hand, can get their fix at Düsseldorf's many well-respected cultural institutions and art locales.

The Top Ten

So you've found yourself in this wondrous new city, near to the end of your journey. What should you see? Where should you go? To the place that has more to offer than any other district of course! The Altstadt is the center of Düsseldorf's fast pace universe, and there is no better way to discover a city than to start in the middle and work your way outward! The Altstadt's stong gravitational pull may be hard to escape, though, as it continues to draw you back into one of the around 260 pubs, many of which serve the city's signature Altbier at any time of the day.

One of the best places to stop in for a glass of the famous Altbier, as well as a hearty feed, is Zum Schiffchen. The restaurant's biggest claim to fame dates back to 1811 when Napoleon ate here with his generals, and was apparently quite satisfied. After ordering a massive meal of the specialties pork knuckle or oxtail (or both) and washing it down with a cool glass of Altbier I guarantee you'll be feeling the same way he did two hundred years back.

The Rheinturm provides a dining experience you won't soon forget, as you're suspended from 240 meters with a 360 degree panoramic view of Düsseldorf! Even if you don't decide to have a meal, or a drink at the cocktail bar, the cheap entrance fee to this remarkable tower is more than worth it for the breath-taking views it provides.

In addition to satisfying your taste buds and appetite, you can satisfy your creative urges at one of the many fine museums within the area. The K21 Standehaus is a notable inclusion which displays a variety of modern artwork that is at the forefront of its genre.

An area just as renowned and ingrained in the culture of Düsseldorf is its wondrous Medianhafen (Media Harbor). Here many world famous architects were entrusted with the task of putting their own mark on the city's skyline, as they were told they had an open canvas to create a modern look for the harbor. This look isn't quite uniform, as the architects all had different building designs in mind, but this only adds to the appeal as when they are put together the buildings all complement each other exquisitely.

Either walk through and under the various buildings yourself, or take a guided tour of the area to learn a bit more about their design.

To connect you between these two main areas, you can't go any other route other than via the Rhine embankment promenade, commonly accepted as one of the most beautiful esplanades in the world. In the summer this strip gains a Mediterranean feel to it as people sit, stand and play along the banks eating, drinking and frolicking in the sun.

Just as 'the Mö' is the area for big name shopping in Hamburg, 'the Kö' is the equivalent, affectionately named place to be in Düsseldorf. Königsallee, like its sister street in Hamburg, is more than just a street to shop on, though, as it represents the elegant lifestyle code most locals aspire to live by, and the sophisticated charm that the city holds so dear. You" find all the big names of fashion in this strip, and might get a sneak peak at some trends that haven't hit anywhere else in the world just yet.

If you're a lover of specialty cars, the Classic Remise Düsseldorf will provide you with an unforgettable day. With pristine, shiny vintage cars stacked from wall to wall, you won't know exactly where to look as you drool over their freshly polished bonnets. If you see something which particularly takes your fancy (and more importantly you can afford it) you can even drive it right out the door!

What you could say is another classic (although a little bit older than any car) is the Schloss Benrath. This extravagant palace is comparable Wes Anderson's Grand Budapest Hotel, with an exquisite pink and purple facade making it truly unique. With a pond at one side and an adorable garden at the other, you'll feel envious that you can't live here yourself.

Take a step back in time to readjust from this modern, chic metropolis by visiting the historical Kaiserwerth area. North of the city and on the Rhine, here you'll find a vast variety of very old stone buildings, and even some ruins for you to explore. This attraction is great for a small excursion any time of the year.

Chapter 10: Cologne

As we sadly arrive at the end of our German adventure, in many ways we could say that the best has been saved for last! Cologne, or Köln in German, is a city in a league of its very own, establishing traditions and customs not found anywhere else within the country, yet maintaining the warm, welcoming atmosphere that all of Germany's fine cities possess.

It is here you'll find some of the biggest celebrations in the whole of the country, as when Karneval roles around each year, the city transforms from a quaint, reserved city into a raging, wild festival. Outside of this period you can still have a jolly time year-round at any of Cologne's unique beer halls.

As you drift about the city you'll pass many jagged, dark, medieval churches and structures, in stark contrast to the care-free liberal citizens that will acknowledge you with a smile and a wave. Cologne will accept and embrace you with open arms, and if you allow yourself to do the same back, it will become your German home away from home.

The Top Ten

The first mention must, of course, go to the impressive Kölner Dom. This cathedral is widely regarded as one of the most visited tourist attractions in the whole of Germany, let alone Cologne! It's not hard to see why, as you stare up at this gargantuan building in wonder, you'll feel as if you're an ant staring at a giant. If you're brave enough you can even ascend the countless steps to the very top, from which you will see an amazing, unobstructed view out over the whole of the beautiful city that is Cologne.

One of the prominent sights you will see from atop the Dom is the River Rhine. This river, which runs directly through the city (and much of Germany), provides a great stretch to walk along and view the rest of the cityscape. You can even partake in a river cruise which will give you an even greater view of Cologne's many highlights.

As you get a little further North of the river, toward the Cologne Cathedral, you will find one of Cologne's more recent traditions - one which displays the romanticism of the River Rhine. Hohenzollern Bridge provides couples with an opportunity to showcase their love for one another, as it is now covered with padlocks of all colors, sizes and shapes (mostly love hearts) engraved with the words "Ich Liebe Dich".

If you didn't take in enough of Cologne from above at the Dom, or get enough of the beautiful River Rhine, check out the Cologne Cable Car. This gondola ride was the first in Europe to go across a river and provides a unique panoramic view of Cologne not to be seen elsewhere. It also provides great entertainment value, as it goes directly over a spa which constantly has nudist lazing about - no matter what the weather!

For something a little more civilized, be sure to check out the Museum Ludwig. It boasts an extensive collection of modern art, one of the largest collections of Picasso in Europe and many works from Andy Warhol. The museum is just one of 36 museums in the city, alongside over 100 galleries, illustrating that Cologne is a truly cultural city.

One of such museums, with a sensually delightful twist, is the Fragrance Museum. If you have ever wondered how the delightful smell that comes from all the big name perfumes is produced, this museum provides a detailed insight into every step involved. It also highlights exactly why Cologne is known as the 'Father of Modern Perfumery'.

To take a look back into the history of the city which predates Germany itself, back to a time when Romans occupied what is now Cologne, there is one lone structure which provides such retrospect. The city gates have stood for around 2000 years, and are in surprisingly good condition considering their age.

As you walk the city, be sure to take a gander down Hohe Strasse, the main shopping strip in Cologne. Forever flooded with people, it provides everything you could want to buy - if you can maneuver the crowds - and is connected to many of the other main streets.

For a more laid-back experience, the Belgian Quarter provides a less mainstream option to shop for some more extravagant items.

Quality is exceeds quantity here, and even the historic buildings which most of the shops are housed in reflect this sentiment.

After all of your walking around, gawking at various must-see sights and shopping until you drop - why not drop yourself onto a stool at one of Cologne's many fine, unique drinking establishments. Cologne boasts its very own type of beer (of which the citizens are vocally proud) called Kölsch. The best place to taste this specialty is in Früh Brewery, where you will find your small Kölsch glass to be never empty, as is the custom, for as soon as the waiter sees that your glass is empty, he will rush to replace it with yet another ice-cold delicious beer.

Conclusion

Germany is a very diverse country with a lot of magnificent, beautiful and awe-inspiring things to see and do. Unfortunately for most people, seeing the whole of Germany's amazing landscape from top to bottom isn't a realistic option.

What I hope to have achieved with this book is to have provided you with a guide how to get the most out of Germany in a limited amount of time. I would encourage you to stay here for as long as possible and soak up everything the country has to offer, but if you can't, just make sure that you don't miss any of the cities I've mentioned and try to get to each of the attractions I've mentioned.

If you can make this round trip of Germany and get to all of the sights I've mentioned, I can guarantee you that you will have had the experience of a lifetime, and will have captured a significant glimpse of Germany's culture, lifestyle, landscape, architectural magnificence and their wonderful people.

I have no doubt that you will return at some stage in the future, hungry to see more of the rich, beautiful and inspiring country that is Germany.

Made in the USA
Lexington, KY
02 September 2015